THE POWER OF
PATRIOTISM

Featuring the story of Francis Scott Key

Author
DeLynn Decker

Art Illustrator
Stephen P. Krause

Editor, Layout and Research
Beatrice W. Friel

THE POWER OF
PATRIOTISM

Featuring the story of Francis Scott Key

Advisors
Paul and Millie Cheesman
Mark Ray Davis
Rodney L. Mann, Jr.
Roxanne Shallenberger
Dale T. Tingey

Publisher
Steven R. Shallenberger

Director and Correlator
Lael J. Woodbury

AN EAGLE SYSTEMS
INTERNATIONAL
PUBLICATION
ANTIOCH, CALIFORNIA

The Power of Patriotism
Copyright © 1981 by
PowerTales
Eagle Systems International
P.O. Box 1229
Antioch, California 94509

ISBN: 0-911712-84-4

Library of Congress Catalog No.: 81-50387

First Edition

Lithographed in USA by
COMMUNITY PRESS, INC.

Dedicated to the citizens of the United States of America in fond
hopes that they too will show their love for their country.

FRANCIS SCOTT KEY

Francis Scott Key was born 1 August 1779 on a large Maryland plantation. His father, John Ross Key, was a prominent merchant and lawyer who gave young Francis his first taste of patriotism in the thrilling stories he told of the recent American Revolution. From his mother, Anne, Francis developed a strong faith in God, which he exercised throughout his life. Bible study and daily family prayer were childhood habits he later instituted into his own family.

Called Frank by friends, young Key had one sister, Anne, who was three years younger. Isolated from other children by distance, the two became close friends and often explored and played together by springs near their mansion. Throughout his life these springs remained a favorite place of relaxation and peace. Key received his formal schooling in Annapolis, Maryland. After seven years of study he graduated as valedictorian from St. John's College.

Having a keen intellect and a love of books, Key's natural course was to study law. In 1800 he was admitted to the Frederick County Bar at the age of 21. He married Mary Tayloe Lloyd in 1802. They became parents of 11 children.

Key moved to Georgetown in 1805 and assumed his uncle's law practice there. About a year later he had the opportunity of defending two men before John Marshall of the United States Supreme Court. His strong, articulate defense won him the acquittal of his clients and gave him a reputation for being a formidable opponent.

Deeply spiritual, Francis was devoted to his parish and paid a tenth of his income to it. He felt strongly that religion and love of country were closely tied together. In a letter to a cousin he stated:

Until a man becomes seriously and strongly impressed with religious sentiments, until he believes *in his heart* that Jesus Christ is his Lord and Master, and joins in the earnest and eloquent application of the converted Paul, 'Lord! what would'st Thou have me do?' his course through life will neither be safe nor pleasant. . . .

In the spring of 1814 Key joined the Georgetown light artillery in defending the Atlantic coast from English warships. Later he served as an aid to General Walter Smith. It was in this capacity that he aided in the escape of President and Mrs. Madison when the Redcoats stormed the Presidential Mansion.

About that time Dr. William Beanes, an intimate friend of Key, was taken prisoner by the English. With his careful preparation and eloquence Key was able to secure Beanes' release from General Ross. Before they were allowed to return to Baltimore, however, they witnessed the British attack of Fort McHenry. It was this stirring experience which led to the writing of what later became the national anthem of the United States of America, "The Star-Spangled Banner."

In 1833 Key became the United States District Attorney for the District of Columbia. He was a man of passion and principle; he gave his fervent all to the causes he believed in. He was known as a man who deplored slavery and the violation of human rights. He valued education and the spirit of commitment. He was good-humored, enthusiastic, and dutiful. He showed his love for his country by using his talents in its behalf, by serving his fellow Americans, and by serving his God. A true patriot, he died on 11 January 1843 at the age of 63. The following story is based on historical facts in his life.

I'm Quinn, the quill pen. Of course everyone knows that pens can't really talk, but let's just pretend that I can. I may look like an ordinary old pen to you, but I once had a friend who thought I was very special. In fact, I helped him write a song that became famous! I'll bet you've even heard it or sung it yourself, but more about that later. My friend's name was Francis Scott Key, and it all started—but wait! Come back in time with me, and I'll let you see for yourself.

On a warm summer day in Maryland ten-year-old Francis Scott Key sat on a stool in an old flour mill. The year was 1789. Francis, called Frank by friends, was listening to Colonel Normand Bruce tell about his adventures in the Revolutionary War. Colonel Bruce had served under General George Washington, who had just become the first president of the United States.

"Tell me again about the time you nearly got caught," asked Frank.

"Well," said the Colonel, his blue eyes bright, "there were several times we barely escaped. Why, I remember the time we stopped for a bite to eat at a farmhouse. We left our guns and supplies in a pile on the floor when we sat down to eat. All of a sudden we heard horses coming! Quick as a wink the four of us slipped out the back and hid in the smokehouse!"

9

Frank's eyes grew big.

"Didn't it *smell* in the smokehouse? It does in ours."

The old soldier chuckled, wrinkling his nose as he remembered.

"Yes, son, it did smell. But we were so glad to find a place to hide that it didn't bother us much."

The slender, blue-eyed boy squirmed on his seat.

"But Colonel! All your things were still in the house! What happened when the soldiers came?"

"That's a good question, Frank," said the Colonel, taking a draw on his pipe. "We were in such a hurry to get out of the house that we forgot everything else. But, lucky for us, the lady remembered. Before the soldiers got to the door, she ran over and covered up what we'd left with her long skirts. Then she stood there the whole time they searched her house."

"Wow," Frank said softly. "What would've happened if they'd found what she was hiding?"

"One thing for sure—it wouldn't have been very pleasant. For her *or* for us."

"Why did she do it, Colonel? What made her take such a chance?" asked Frank.

"Well, I think she cared more about freedom than she cared about being safe. She knew we were fighting so that America could be free from King George. And I think she wanted her children to grow up in a country where a leader didn't control everything they did. So she did what she could to make this a place where people can choose for themselves."

"She really showed her love for her country, didn't she, sir?"

"Yes, son, as much as any soldier I fought with. You might say, she was a real patriot."

Frank sighed happily as he picked up a broom. He liked the warm, musty smells of the flour mill. He had spent many boyhood hours there listening to stories of his friend's daring adventures.

That evening Frank lay thinking in front of the fireplace. His mother was quietly mending. His seven-year-old sister, Anne, was not so quietly working on her embroidery.

"You know what I'd like to be when I grow up?" said Frank as he absently scratched his dog's ears.

"No, what?" answered Anne, looking up from the knot she was trying to untie.

"I'd like to do something really great for America. I want to be a patriot."

"Maybe you'll get some ideas when you go to Annapolis," said Anne.

Frank was going to live with an aunt and uncle while he attended school in Annapolis. His mother had taught him to read and write, and he was already good at rhymes and music. But now it was time for him to learn other things that his mother could not teach him. The school he would be attending was called St. John's College.

Mrs. Key looked up from her mending.

"You know," she said, "maybe you're both in too much of a hurry. You have to learn one step at a time before you can be really good at anything. Learning takes time. You wouldn't have so much trouble with your needlework if you would be more patient, Anne."

Anne looked at the knots and loose threads in her embroidery.

"But it's so hard to go slow when I want to get finished!" she fretted.

"Do you think your father would have become a good lawyer if he had rushed through his studies?" asked Mrs. Key. "He had to spend a lot of time reading the laws and learning what they mean. He had to do that before he could use then wisely."

"But what about me?" said Frank. "What do I need to learn so I can be a patriot?"

"Well, you want to stand up for America," said his mother. "Have you thought about what America stands for? Most of all, America stands for freedom. What does that mean to you, Frank?"

"I think freedom means you have a chance to do what you want to do. Colonel Bruce says some countries tell their people what to do all the time. And they have to do it," said Frank.

"He's right, dear," said Mrs. Key. "The freedom to choose for yourself is called freedom of choice. It means you can do or be what you want. Another freedom that goes along with freedom of choice is freedom of speech. That means it is safe to say what you think is true. In some countries people are put in prison if their government doesn't like what they say."

There was more to it than Frank thought. He loved hearing about his country. Someday he would find a way to become a real patriot.

Just before Frank left for Annapolis, Anne gave him a quill pen.

"This is to help you remember to write home," she said.

As they drove away in the carriage, Frank looked closely at the pen. It seemed to wink at him. He felt better right away.

"I think I'll call you Quinn," he said. "If I make you my friend, maybe I won't be so lonesome for home."

Now Frank knew the quill pen wasn't really alive, but he imagined that it was his friend. When Quinn seemed to talk to him, Frank knew it was really his own thoughts he was hearing. But somehow it made things more fun to have an imaginary friend along.

THINK ABOUT IT

1. Why is it better to learn things one step at a time?
2. What are some countries where the people do not have freedom of speech?
3. How do you think the people feel who live there?

DEVELOPING TALENTS AND CHARACTER

At school Frank's favorite classes were languages and drama. His best friends were Daniel Murray and John Shaw. They often went ice skating or exploring together. The three of them were also known for playing practical jokes. Once Frank even galloped around the school yard on a cow just to make friends laugh. It was a good thing his grandmother lived nearby to help keep him straight.

Mrs. Ann Arnold Key, the mother of Frank's father, had been blinded while trying to save some people trapped in a burning house. Frank thought she was brave and wonderful. He loved to visit her.

"Guess what I found out today, Grandmother!" he burst in one day after school. "You know that giant tulip poplar on the grounds of St. John's? Well, it's hundreds of years old, and all kinds of exciting things have happened there! The settlers signed an Indian treaty under it, and Continental soldiers even camped there during the Revolution! What do you think of that?"

"I think you are running over with enthusiasm, that's what I think," Mrs. Key said. "But I'm glad to have you come. You always cheer up my day, Francis."

One day he told his grandmother of his dream of being a patriot.

"But the treaties are already signed, and the war is over," he complained. "What do you think *I* can do?"

Wrapping her shawl closer, Mrs, Key answered thoughtfully, "You have a special way with words, Francis. I think it is one of your gifts. Perhaps the time will come when you can write something for America. Or maybe you will use words in a way that will inspire others to become better Americans. That would be a very good thing to do. You don't have to risk your life to become a patriot, dear."

Frank sighed impatiently. If only he could do something now!

Then, on the morning of March 25, 1791, when Frank was twelve years old, something very special happened.

"Get up!" called Quinn, tickling Frank's toes. "Today is the day the President is coming!"

Frank leaped out of bed and scrambled into his clothes.

"How could I forget!" he said. "George Washington is coming to St. John's. And he's one of the greatest patriots of all!"

"Don't forget me!" cried Quinn. "When he says something important, you'll need me to write it down!"

The students at St. John's listened carefully as President Washington spoke to them.

"When you take up your careers, I hope that all of you will bring credit to this school because of your good character and conduct," he said.

"What does 'character' mean?" whispered Quinn from Frank's coat pocket.

"It means the way a person acts and thinks. A person with strong character keeps his word," said Frank. "He stands up for what he believes. 'Conduct' means how you behave."

Just then John passed him a note.

"Look at his teeth," it said. "My father says they are wooden. That's why he talks like that!"

Quinn poked Frank.

"Your character may turn out all right," he said, "but with that John Shaw around you'd better keep an eye on your conduct!"

In 1796, when he was seventeen, Frank received the degree of Bachelor of Arts. That was like a high school diploma today. He was also chosen to be the valedictorian, the person who gives the farewell speech at the graduation ceremony. It was quite an honor, and his family was very proud.

THINK ABOUT IT

1. What can you do to develop a stronger character?
2. What kind of character traits would you like to have? Some examples are honesty, loyalty, cheerfulness, dependability.

THE NATION GOES TO WAR

After graduating from St. John's, Frank studied law with an uncle, Philip Barton Key. He still lived in Annapolis, and by this time he had become quite tall and handsome with his dark hair and blue eyes. It wasn't long before he noticed a charming young lady named Mary Lloyd.

Mary, whose nickname was Polly, was only sixteen. She didn't like Frank very much at first. She made fun of the love poems he wrote to her.

"If you don't stop writing these silly rhymes," she told him, "I'm going to use them to curl my hair!" And sure enough, when she saw him from her window, she would point to her curls and smile. Poor Frank!

But by the time Frank finished his law studies, Polly had changed her mind. They were married in 1802. Then they moved to Frederick Town, Maryland, where Frank began to practice law.

The budding little nation of the United States was having trouble with England during these years. England was using her seamen to fight against France in a war. This meant she didn't have enough men left to run the merchant ships that took supplies to other countries.

American ships began to deliver cotton and tobacco to the West Indies and Europe. England was unhappy about losing the trading business. She tried to keep the American ships from trading by blocking the foreign ports. America did not like England interfering. On June 18, 1812, the United States declared war on England.

"I'm afraid we have jumped into war without really thinking," Frank told Quinn. "Many people will die in this war. I am just not sure a few trading routes are worth the loss of their lives."

Discouraged with what was happening with the country, Frank turned his attention to his family. When each child was born, he planted a tiny garden for it. The plants and flowers were arranged to spell out the name of the child.

Frank taught his children to read the Bible and to love America.

"I hope you will become like George Washington," he told them. "A true patriot serves his country and his God."

"That's right," said Polly. "If you can make life better for even one person, it will help make happier families. And families are what our country is made of. It would be a good thing for all of us to think about how we can make life better for each other."

Soon British ships began to sneak into American harbors and cause trouble. The British planned to land their troops, the Redcoats, and take over Washington, D.C., the capital of the United States. At this time Frank was involved in the war effort. His duty was to protect President James Madison and Mrs. Madison. One night he warned them that England's General Ross and his troops were on their way to the President's Mansion. President and Mrs. Madison fled to Virginia for safety.

A little later Frank became worried about a friend. "You know, Quinn," he said, "I haven't heard anything from my good friend Dr. Beanes. I am afraid the Redcoats took him prisoner when they came through."

Dr. William Beanes had indeed been taken prisoner. He was being held aboard the English ship, the *Tonnant*. Frank obtained permission from President Madison to contact the English leader, General Ross, in Dr. Beanes' behalf. Wishing to be as prepared as possible, Frank first visited the wounded English soldiers Dr. Beanes had treated. They were glad to write letters saying they had received good care from the doctor. Frank hoped the letters would help persuade General Ross to let Dr. Beanes go.

When he was ready, Frank and another lawyer, John B. Skinner, set out on a small ship with a white flag. They were going to find the *Tonnant*.

___

THINK ABOUT IT

1. What are some ways you can serve your country and your God?
2. What could you do to make life better for someone? Choose someone in your family. What are some things you could do to make that person happy?

A PATRIOT AT LAST

They found the British ship near the mouth of the Potomac River and were taken on board. Then General Ross agreed to see them. Frank knew that what he was going to say might be the most important speech he ever made, for it involved a man's life.

"General Ross, sir," he began, "we are here to ask for mercy on behalf of Dr. Beanes. He is a man whose heart and services have no boundaries. He has served both English and Americans, the slave and the free. When your wounded were left behind, he went to them with medicine and care. Here are letters from your own men telling of his kindness to them. He is not a soldier, but an old man now. He will bring no harm to you in this war. We ask you to take the chains from him, that he may go on doing his good work."

General Ross had listened with respect. He knew that Frank's words were true.

"You have spoken well," he said. "A man would be fortunate to have you for a friend. Perhaps you have saved this old man's life. I have decided that he may return with you, but not yet. We are going to attack Baltimore, and all of you must stay with us until it is over."

"Oh no!" exclaimed Quinn. "Now we're going to be in the middle of a battle!"

But they weren't to be in the middle of it. They were returned to their own ship with a group of British marines to guard them. From there they could watch the attack, but they could not give a warning.

"How did you know General Ross wouldn't just capture you, too?" asked Quinn.

"It was a chance I had to take," replied Frank. "Dr. Beanes' safety was the most important thing to consider."

"Your grandmother was right," said Quinn, beaming. "It was the way you used words that made General Ross decide to let him go! You really *have* become a patriot!"

While the British were preparing for the battle, Mrs. Mary Pickersgill was sewing a flag that would soon become famous. To encourage their men, American General John Stricker and Commodore Barney had asked her to make a huge flag. It had fifteen red and white stripes with fifteen white

stars on a blue background. She used four hundred yards of material. When it was finished the flag was raised on a very tall pole behind the guns of Fort McHenry. It could be seen for miles.

On Monday morning, September 12, 1814, the British soldiers left their ships and started for land. They were about ten miles from Fort McHenry, which protected the city of Baltimore. General Ross ordered the ships to begin firing.

"Look at that!" cried Quinn. "Their cannon fire almost reaches the fort!"

"Indeed," said Frank seriously. "And our shells are not strong enough to touch the British ships."

All that day Frank, Dr. Beanes, and John Skinner watched the battle through binoculars. They were miles away, but they could still see the flag Mrs. Pickersgill had made.

"See that flag?" said one of their guards. "You'd better take a good look at it tonight. Tomorrow you won't be seeing it!"

That night the sky was bright with the blazing red lights of rockets and bursting bombs. Shortly after midnight British Admiral Cochrane sent several warships up the river. They needed to get closer in order to capture Fort McHenry.

Frank and his friends watched helplessly as the ships moved quietly past them.

"Isn't there anything we can do?" asked Quinn. "If we don't warn them, Fort McHenry won't have a chance."

And so it seemed. But there was an alert American patrol close to the riverbank.

"Listen!" said one of the patroling soldiers. "I think I hear boats creaking!" They stood perfectly still. It *was* the sound of boats moving in the river! Quickly they set fire to a haystack. That would give an alarm to the soldiers closer to the fort. They were watching from behind the ramparts (high dirt banks they had built). Now, in the glow of the burning haystack, they could see the shadows of the approaching British ships. They still had a chance!

Frank knew this was a very important battle. If the British captured Baltimore, they might be able to win the war. He stayed up all night watching bombs burst all around him.

"How long is the firing going to go on?" asked Quinn. "Surely it can't last much longer."

The dark of the night began to change into the gray of dawn. Frank turned the binoculars toward the fort. It was still hard to see through the smoke of the cannons.

"It's there!" he cried. "The flag is safe! That means they haven't taken Fort McHenry!"

At the shoreline Redcoats were climbing into boats and returning to their warships for safety. The fighting was over.

Frank's heart was full of excitement and gratitude. He pulled an old letter from his coat pocket.

"Help me, Quinn," he said. "This is the only paper I have. I must write this down while I am feeling this way!" And he began to write down his thoughts about the night, the flag, and the battle.

The British guards soon returned to their own ship, and Frank and his friends started back to Baltimore. Frank worked on his rhyme along the way. That night he finished it at an inn. The story he told began with a question:

"O say can you see by the dawn's early light
What so proudly we hail'd at the twilight's last gleaming,
Whose broad stripes and bright stars through the perilous fight
O'er the ramparts we watch'd were so gallantly streaming?
And the rocket's red glare, the bombs bursting in air,
Gave proof through the night that our flag was still there,
O say does that star-spangled banner yet wave
O'er the land of the free and the home of the brave?

"On the shore dimly seen through the mists of the deep,
Where the foe's haughty host in dread silence reposes,
What is that which the breeze, o'er the towering steep,
As it fitfully blows, half conceals, half discloses?
Now it catches the gleam of the morning's first beam,
In full glory reflected now shines in the stream,
'Tis the star-spangled banner—O long may it wave
O'er the land of the free and the home of the brave!

"And where is that band who so vauntingly swore,
That the havoc of war and the battle's confusion
A home and a country should leave us no more?
Their blood has wash'd out their foul footsteps pollution,
No refuge could save the hireling and slave
From the terror of flight or the gloom of the grave,
And the star-spangled banner in triumph doth wave
O'er the land of the free and the home of the brave."

In the last stanza Frank wrote the idea behind what has
become the motto of our American government: "In God
we trust."

"O thus be it ever when freemen shall stand
Between their lov'd home and the war's desolation!
Blest with vict'ry and peace may the heav'n rescued land
Praise the power that hath made and preserved us a nation!
Then conquer we must, when our cause it is just,
And this be our motto—'In God is our trust,'
And the star-spangled banner in triumph shall wave
O'er the land of the free and the home of the brave."

The rhyme Frank wrote was set to music and became a popular song called "The Defense of Fort McHenry." The title was later changed to "The Star-Spangled Banner." In 1931 it became the official national anthem of the United States of America.

And so it was that Frank became a patriot. He risked his life to save his friend, Dr. Beanes. Using his talent with words, he was able to talk General Ross into letting Dr. Beanes go free. And the poem he wrote has inspired millions of Americans who love their country. The next time you hear "The Star-Spangled Banner," perhaps you will remember the exciting event in history that it is describing. And someday maybe you will have a chance to show your love for your country by using your talents. Then you will be a patriot, too!